DISCOVER
The Laws of Motion

by Barbara Brannon

Table of Contents

Introduction

Newton studied how things move. Newton studied things in **motion**. Newton studied the **laws** of motion.

▲ Sir Isaac Newton studied motion.

laws

force

motion

object

pulls

pushes

See the Glossary
on page 22.

3

What Is the First Law of Motion?

The **object** begins to move. The object continues to move.

▲ The water is in motion.

The ball begins to move. The ball continues to move.

▲ The ball is in motion.

Newton studied objects at rest. The objects do not move.

▲ The ball does not move.

The clock begins to move. The clock continues to move.

▲ The clock is in motion.

The swing begins to move. The swing continues to move.

▲ The swing is in motion.

What Is the Second Law of Motion?

A **force pushes**. The object moves.

▲ This leaf moves.

A force pushes harder. The object moves faster.

▲ These leaves move faster.

A force pushes. The object moves.

▲ This wall moves.

A force pushes harder. The object moves faster.

▲ This wall moves faster.

Did You Know?

Gravity is a force. Gravity makes objects move faster.

▲ Gravity makes the skier move faster.

A force **pulls**. The object moves.

▲ This plow moves.

A force pulls harder. The object moves faster.

▲ This plow moves faster.

A force pulls. The object moves.

▲ This suitcase moves.

A force pulls harder. The object moves faster.

▲ This suitcase moves faster.

What Is the Third Law of Motion?

An object pushes forward.

▲ The shuttle pushes forward.

An object moves backward.

An object pushes forward.

▲ The water pushes forward.

An object pushes backward.

▲ The hose pushes backward.

An object pushes forward.

▲ The paddle pushes forward.

An object pushes backward.

▲ The water pushes backward.

Newton studied why objects move. Newton studied how objects move. Newton studied the laws of motion.

Concept Map

Motion

What Is the First Law of Motion?

object begins to move

object continues to move

What Is the Second Law of Motion?

force pushes

force pushes harder

object moves

object moves faster

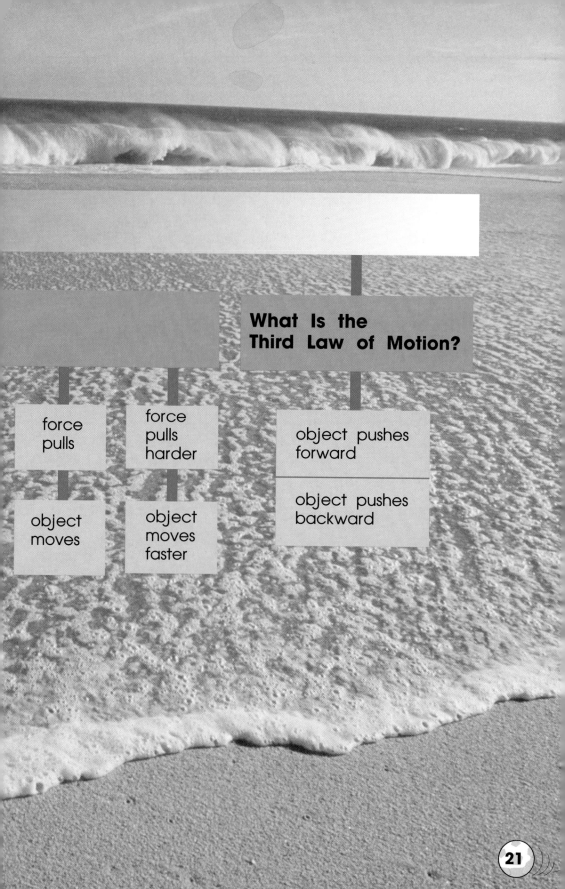

What Is the Third Law of Motion?

force
pulls

object
moves

force
pulls
harder

object
moves
faster

object pushes
forward

object pushes
backward

Glossary

force a power that makes an object move

*A **force** pulls.*

laws rules about how things work

*Newton studied the **laws** of motion.*

motion the act of moving

*Newton studied things in **motion**.*

object matter that you can see or touch

*The **object** moves.*

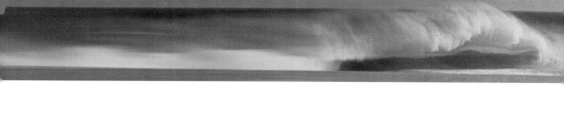

pulls moves an object toward

*A force **pulls**.*

pushes moves an object away from

*A force **pushes** harder.*

Index